Elisabeth Mandt

Intuitive Intelligence

Welcoming the Guest

ISBN: 1-4610-8998-0
ISBN-13: 9781461089988

DEDICATION

This book is dedicated to my daughter Dominique
and to all who seek.

CONTENTS

ACKNOWLEDGMENTS

So how do intuitive messages capture our imagination and translate into inspiration and how does inspiration turn into action?

It was on a Tuesday towards the end of July 2010 when I was on my way to work. As I merged unto the freeway, I suddenly had this distinct excitement in my chest: I need to write a book. So what type of book, I asked? At that moment when I asked I did not expect an immediate answer. After all I consider myself a ponder type of person, letting messages slow-simmer into my awareness. Not so this day! I clearly was "told" this will be a book about intuition. Next thing I got was" INTUITIVE INTELLIGENCE". Was that the title? I asked. Yes, the answer came. It will be a small book on your intuitive moments and how we all are intuitive.

OK, so I immediately set to work, took out my cell phone (yes, while driving…) and called the first person that came to mind. I shook my head in disbelief, thinking: what will Sandy say when she hears this. Sandy is a friend I worked with years ago; she is a walking and talking intuitive. She and I have not talked for 5 years- we each needed to do our own thing. And yet, when I heard her voice say hello, I introduced myself and proceeded to invite her to contribute her own intuitive moments to this book. Without hesitation came the answer: "Sure, I'll do it, come to my house and bring a tape recorder…"

That's how this book came into being…

Excitement was building further as I contacted my friend Alisa. I have known Alisa for a long time and have instantly felt connected to her the first time the two of us met in a doctor's office. As I pulled into the parking lot at work I had this book fully sketched out in my mind…

I feel grateful to Alisa, Sandy, my own family, especially my husband and daughter who have been so patiently tolerating an overflowing kitchen table for the last three months.

I am also grateful to the unseen and yet very present divine guides and my guardian angel.

Chapter 1

WHAT IS INTUITION?

When the body functions spontaneously
That is called instinct
When the soul functions spontaneously,
That is called intuition.
They are alike and yet
Far away from each other.
Instinct is of the body- the gross;
And intuition is of the soul—the subtle.
And between the two is the mind, the expert,
Which never functions spontaneously.
Instinct is deeper than intellect.
Intuition is higher than intellect.
Both are beyond the intellect....

Osho

The word intuition comes from the Latin *intueri*, meaning to consider, to look on. This intuitive "look on" implies something deeper than simple perception and is best described as apperception, the ability to "take hold of" knowledge in one glance.

The Webster's Unabridged Dictionary sums up intuition as "the immediate knowing or learning of something without the conscious use of reasoning; instantaneous apperception." Simply stated, intuition is direct knowledge.

In the last decades the term *emotional intelligence* has been associated with the ability to perceive, assimilate, process and correctly interpret and apply our own emotions. Emotional intelligence is now well recognized as the ability to decipher the meaning of emotions and their relationships, and to reason and problem solve on the basis of them.

In contrast, the term *social intelligence* was coined by E.L. Thorndike as early as 1920 to describe the skill of understanding and managing other people.

So what is Intuition?

From a mystical standpoint intuition is what happens when we receive illumination or enlightenment while steadily looking inward, concentrating with a sense of devotion and a desire to receive understanding and wisdom directly from the divine.

From the esoteric perspective, accessing your intuition means tuning into and correctly interpreting the subtle vibrations of energy you receive. These energetic impulses may be invisible and intangible, yet they are real and we are all capable of accessing this information by paying attention and by learning how to tune in and interpret these subtle impulses.

Intuition is the ability to "listen" between the lines. Intuition also happens at times when a certain sound, whatever it may be- be it a bird chirping or the sound of rain falling unto your roof—is heard. Intuition can be triggered by a smell, a sight, the light falling upon the sidewalk as you walk home from work.

Why do we need to develop intuition? In my opinion intuition connects you to your soul's purpose. It enhances your ability to communicate, make decisions that lead to meaning, avoid senseless spinning-of-the-wheel activities. Intuition helps you clean your slate, removes the mundane dust and noise.

Developing and honoring intuitive intelligence in addition to emotional intelligence brings into your life the advantage of intense, core living. Aside from promoting good communication it makes you more sensitive to the people around you. This sensitivity promotes understanding them better. Intuition makes you far more creative than ever. Intuition helps you tap into and release creative juices you never knew you had.

Finally, intuition has the potential to unlock your healing powers. As you delve deeply into your soul to cancel out negative energy you learn to use positive energy for healing.

Most people believe, however, that INTUITION is a talent. They believe, only the privileged few possess it and even fewer have the ability to fully develop intuitive senses and gain the benefits from its understanding.

Western culture holds the mind and technology in high regard: the quest for knowledge leaves very little room for intuition. We don't encourage our children to recognize, honor and grow intuition. And the children who do express their intuitive intelligence get often silenced...

My friend Sandy was one such child who grew up in a loving family, a church going family. Even as a young child she knew and felt things other members of the family did not. She notes:"There were only a few people I could talk to about the things I saw and experienced. Instinctively I knew who I could and could not talk to. Even my mother could accept a message only when it came from the church. She was so fearful when she heard me talk so as a child I learned not to express my intuition.

In my opinion intuition is this thing that you know you know! You may get a message under a steeple and it is just as accurate as the message you get under a tree or when you sit at the bank of a lake. The source is the same but our society labels it differently. "

Irina Tweedie, author of "Daughter of Fire" and a profound Sufi mystic was once interviewed by Dr. Jeffrey Mishlove for The Intuition Network and said this about intuition: "The higher form of intellect is intuition....Intuition works like a spark, and you see, all the great inventions, all the great discoveries really do not come from the mind. What does the mind do? It calculates it, it prepares the field, and it prepares the cup. But the ultimate spark is always intuition. It may be an apple falling from the tree like in the case of Newton. It may be this little bit of mold, which will one day be penicillin and so on and so forth. The ultimate factor in every invention, in every discovery, is intuition. The mind prepares only the field. The real wisdom, the gnosis comes from the soul. We do not even think with the brain...We think somewhere above our head, in our mental body, and the brain is only transmuting it into words. It's only a kind of computer, a kind of—how shall I say—instrument."

In order to better understand intuition let's look at how our conscious and subconscious mind operates.

The conscious mind analyzes information, thinks and plans and holds short term memory. In contrast the majority, almost 90% of our mental activity comes through the subconscious mind. The subconscious mind operates involuntary functions such as breathing; it holds long term memory, houses emotions and feelings, holds habits, behavioral patterns, relationship dynamics and addictive tendencies. Development stages encode in the subconscious mind, spiritual concepts take hold there and intuition comes through the subconscious mind.

A spiritual teacher, a teacher of awareness and communication, Patricia Sun, was also interviewed by Dr. Mishlove from The Intuitive Network acknowledges that as part of developing our brains fully we must develop the logical mind as well as maturing the intuitive mind. In her estimation the intuitive mind is often misunderstood in our culture. In context of using intuition as a healing agent Patricia states:

" Intuition is soft, it's gentle, it's kind, it's feeling...And if you hold it in a state of respect for the other person and yourself equally, if you equally respect your own feelings and the other person's feelings, then when you communicate it's almost magical. We begin to bond. And that is really what a conscious relationship is."

The right brain is the seat of insights, solutions, and talents.

The left brain is the seat of logic, rational thinking, and thinking in dualities: right versus wrong, polarizing between good and bad, holding judgments.

According to Sun:"Our left brain, the linear mind is immature; the immature linear mind needs to be right, judgmental; it thinks only in duality."

In contrast, the intuitive mind, the right brain thinks in pictures, produces feelings, creates images and sensations in the body. Patricia Sun believes this part of the brain has the capacity to tap into the wisdom of the DIVINE.

I believe in order to access the essence of one's life the universe has given us the gift of intuition. Intuitive intelligence is the way of connecting with the within and the without: it manifests profound growth and boundless creativity.

Chapter 2

ACCESSING YOUR INTUITION

Listen to your intuition.
It will tell you everything you need to know.

Anthony D Angelo

I was born in Romania in a small town called Satchinez in the Western region of Banat, surrounded by flat fields of wheat and corn, pastures filled with cows. Looking back, it was a great place to grow up in a time when Gypsies and their covered wagons showed up on dusty country lanes with their pots and pans and magic.

The ground work for my own intuitive capacity was laid very early on: hiding with a book in a cornfield behind my house or perched on an old walnut tree by the pond, these are moments I remember as peaceful, solitary reflective ones where I felt connected to myself and a far bigger force surrounding me.

My intuitive guidance was however accessed years later...

It was August 1976 I had my first chance at visiting my old home. Homesick, I found myself back in Communist Romania. I haled a "private cab" at the train station in nearby Timisoara- after discovering that the last train to my home town just left. I came to visit from Germany where my parents and younger sister had immigrated to one year prior. Instead of staying overnight in a hotel in the city and waiting to take the train next day I decided to do something different. Very spur of the moment I approached a "private cab", (regular folks offering rides in their own cars to subsidize their meager incomes). With little luggage in tow, just a carry on size suitcase and my purse—I approached the owner of a Dacia and asked him if he would drive me to Satchinez.

"Of course; just you?" he asked. "Yes, just me".

So I settled into the back seat of his car and felt really good about my grown up decision to go home tonight. I was 19, had enough cash and felt worldly.

Initially, the trip was uneventful. I exchanged pleasantries with the driver in Romanian, asked about his family, talked about the weather and slowly the car made its way through dark, quiet and sleepy pastures. I felt relaxed and quiet and at times dozed off. Suddenly, like a jolt of lightning, I knew I was in trouble. A flash of paralyzing fear hit me in my stomach; I sat up, could hardly breathe. This was the kind of fear that keeps you from exhaling—and right at that very moment the driver turned around to me, snickered and said in a quiet but firm voice: "What, are you afraid of me?" "You know, you should be afraid of me…" That's when I opened my mouth and heard myself saying: "Me, afraid of you? Why would I be afraid of you?' I got your tag number and besides, I know I am safe with you being that my father is the police chief in my town. Why would I be afraid of you? You are doing me a favor to give me a ride and I will not tell my father you did this illegally".

He gave me a searching look.

"See, I am not afraid of you…" With that I sank back into the back seat, my heart in my throat. That changed everything: the man turned face forward again and kept driving without saying a word. Later he explained how he had to earn extra money and driving people around in the evenings helped him raise his children. I assured him I understood. The car finally pulled unto Main Street of my home town barely illuminated by one lonely street light at the corner. He asked for 750 Lei, (a train ticket cost 18 Lei in those days). This was an outrageous amount of money and I knew I needed to remain cool. I retrieved my luggage, counted 350 Lei into the open palm of his hand and with a voice I barely recognized I said: "Turn your car around in three moves and go back to the city. Don't get any funny ideas; I got your license plate number…I will not tell my father if you get out of here this very instance." He grabbed the money, got into his car and with wheels squealing in this quiet night, whisked it around and sped off. Once his tail lights disappeared behind the corner I started shaking, my knees wobbled. I sat down on my suitcase in the middle of the gravel street.

My first intuitive moment in action…it saved my life!!! And I was "home".

My friend Alisa was similarly guided by her intuition when she found herself in the middle of an unusual encounter. Here is her recollection of her own intuitive guidance.

Many years, I have hurt my arm in a fall at a store I have been sent to physical therapy. The therapist I have met there was wonderful; it turns out I have been sent to her not so much for my body to be healed but God has sent me to her to connect with her. And we have had this connection and started talking about the Masters, about spiritual things. And even though I went back for the physical healing I knew I went back for that spiritual connection, for that love and the friendship we have formed. We have remained friends over the years. Sometimes we would not talk or see each other for years but that connection remained. We could just think of each other and we were connected. I believe God kept bringing us back together.

This lady wanted a baby so badly and she did everything she was meant to do and at some point said: I know there is a baby out there…but it is not coming through my body.

So one day, as I am shopping at a mall, having a good day, it was time for lunch. So I walk over to the yoghurt shop and behind the counter is a highly pregnant lady, turns out she was having twins. She is saying to another lady behind the counter—not paying attention to me, the customer -I am going to give one of my babies away. And I said to her: I want your baby. But the lady said, no, I have already found a family member to give my baby to but you may want to talk to the lady across the hall who is serving lunch over there; she wants to give her baby away, she can't keep her baby.

So I walk across the hall and ask this pregnant lady if we could talk and she agreed to take a break at lunch time. When that moment came I explained to her I have a friend who is waiting to adopt a baby and she said, ok, I will get in touch with you. And she did and this led to my friend adopting this beautiful baby girl.

I believe God sent me to this therapist and God sent me to this lady in the mall for the baby to be brought to her rightful mother in this life time. I had to hurt my shoulder so I would be sent to the therapist so the therapist could help me heal and so that I could find her baby.

I am so glad I listened to my intuition that day as I believe God was preparing this child to find her mommy and daddy and timing was perfect. Timing is always perfect. Divine time is always perfect: it's never too late, it's never too early, it is always exactly right. The moment things need to happen, they will happen. Anytime we rush things, chaos will set in.

So I truly believe on that particular day in the mall the angels were saying: now go over there and talk to that lady, pick up the phone and talk with your friend and help mom and child find each other."

You would never think intuition could help you get back to college, do you?

Well, here is how intuition guided me to enroll in college courses.

Over the years, especially when our daughter was little, I suffered from carpal tunnel syndrome. The numbness and pain was so severe, I was afraid I would drop her when getting up in the middle of the night for her feedings. It became increasingly clear that I needed to pursue another career. But how? Paying for courses can be expensive. So I started praying.

I remember clearly, one day after work driving to a small spiritual gathering at my teacher Betty's house. On the way there I prayed so loud and so intensely I found myself in tears: "Please God open the door, help me go back to school. Please God, show me the way and I promise I will do my work. Please God, shout at me if I don't listen; get my attention, please, and show me the way!!!"

Before our lessons started we chatted a bit. That evening, Amanda, one of the regular attendees, excitedly declared she had an opportunity to go back to school to pursue an associate's degree. "That will give me a chance to change jobs since I can no longer work in my old line of work..." Her enthusiasm and excitement got my attention. She proceeded to tell me how a government grant would pay for this degree in light of a career restructuring based on her medical condition. I listened closely: "Elisabeth, the meeting with my financial counselor will take place next Thursday and here is the phone number in case you also want to attend. Hope to see you there, Elisabeth, next Thursday".

I knew this was it!

Next Thursday came and I was attending this meeting, I was early. No Amanda in sight. Later on I found out she changed her mind and did not want to pursue this educational opportunity after all. I filled out all the paperwork and was accepted into this grant driven associates degree program. My prayer was answered. I started my 2 year degree on a scholarship that August and slowly pursued my bachelor's degree in psychology followed by my master's degree in social work. Intuitive intelligence paved the way!!!

Yet another similar intuitive guidance came out of the blue:

It was June 21, 2006. My father-in-law just died May 2, 2006. He was one week shy of being 75 years old. My mother-in-law was in the hospital in Orange City, had undergone cyst removal on her spinal cord and was recovering at a skilled nursing home in Deland. That Saturday, my daughter, now 12, and I took ourselves to Deland to clean up the mostly empty house and to decide how to dispose of their furniture.

It was a peaceful hot summer day and we drove the pickup truck carrying empty boxes and cleaning supplies. As I cleared out more trash and started cleaning, their neighbor Rich came over to talk about which pieces of furniture he could possibly sell for us. He knew some families in town who needed furniture. As we walked through the house we placed price tags via yellow sticky notes on individual dressers, hutches and tables. Not much money could be expected, Rich explained in his kind, polite southern way. I knew that and did not expect much either. But we needed to ready the house for renting.

My last stop at assessing prices and attaching stickers was in my father-in-law's office. A dark Ethan Allen desk, chest of drawers and book shelves lined the small room. Now that all his beloved collectibles were safely boxed up, I could actually see the furniture. A sense of sadness overcame me when I heard Rich apologetically explain that especially this type of furniture is not much in demand any more.

As I walked out of the room, right before I switched off the light, I turned around and suddenly I had this vision. I saw this exact same furniture, whitewashed in a Nantucket style vacation home.

I quickly headed down the hall, and saying good bye to Rich, closed the front door. Within minutes, without attaching any more price tags, I collected my daughter and started on the two hour long drive home.

Dominique, cranky and tired, soon fell asleep on the passenger seat of my pickup truck. As I kept driving I could not shake the vision of all this furniture white washed in a Nantucket style house.

"But we are not Nantucket type vacation folks, I argued with my vision. We love taking vacations in North Carolina…" Just as you would flip a switch these pieces of furniture appeared in a mountain house in NC. "O boy, how am I going to tell Hans about this? He is very realistic, not too eager to follow intuitive hunches…"

He was watching a car race or a football game on TV and was glad to see us back home.

"How would you like to own a vacation home in North Carolina?" I carefully opened the conversation. In order to avoid a definite "no" I immediately asked him to keep an open mind and proceeded to tell him about my vision. To my utter surprise Hans got off the sofa, went into his office and minutes later brought me a list of houses from real estate ads on the internet: houses for sale in Western North Carolina.

The first picture showed a mountain house with a sweeping porch overlooking mountains, a peaceful valley with barns, cows and a few scattered houses. The covered porch on the other side was cozy. We looked at each other, and then looked at these pictures again and next day contacted Caldwell Banker real estate company to book a showing.

On the long weekend of the 4th of July we were up there and as we walked up the driveway to this house it felt so right. Just to assure ourselves this house was it we looked at another half dozen houses. And at the end we returned to the first house again, tired but very convinced we found our house. Peacefully waiting for us was this house we have since grown to love and call "our friend" who has been in our family since Labor Day of 2006.

Almost all of grandpa's furniture made it into the house, not one stitch is white washed, though. It all started with a faint feeling that evolved into a sketchy vision of a Nantucket house and here we are four years later having spent many fun family vacations with our friend.

Our steps were led to our friend by intuition...

ൟ

Chapter 3
INTUITION: IMAGINATION AT WORK

Imagination is more important than knowledge.

Albert Einstein

Intuition teaches us profound lessons that are beyond the grasp of our normal mind. In your imagination, everything is possible. Imagination is the playground where you can envision new ideas and beliefs, where you can modify these beliefs, plant new ideas that will manifest a new reality and dissolve a reality no longer needed.

Imagery and symbols are the language of your imagination.

So, can you and should you trust your imagination?

Vivid imagination brings a rich sensory input and a variety of emotional undertones to your intuitional insights. Imagination is your friend bringing you messages from your soul.

Imagination can increase your self-expression and improve your creativity.

So are you living your life to your highest intuitive and creative potential?

You may test this by naming five things you would want to do if money were no option. Pay attention to what pops into your mind as an image and a desire.

Intuitive information may show up via a book, a movie, running into an old friend. To test your imagination, grab a canvas and paint. Allow your creativity to show up. So what, if you cannot paint; what if the sunset you imagined looks more like an orange mess!!!

...If you ignore your intuition it will go to sleep. When you allow your imagination to come alive, when you bake a cake, when you paint, when you create a haiku, you come alive.

When you dance like there is no tomorrow, in abandon, without caring if your dance steps are correct, you feel alive. Switch up your routine, try something new, go out into unchartered territory and enjoy being frivolous, irrelevant and impulsive. You suddenly come alive!!!

Here is the Haiku I created one evening through automatic writing:

Chambers of my Heart
Feeling like entering the chambers of my heart-
Veil upon veil removed-
Deeper and deeper into the core of my being-
Finally at home in this universe;
Breathing and bowing down;
Inviting all the Ancients to be present
Presence: take a seat in my Heart
Like the early morning mist over the lake
At the foot of the mountain.
Sitting in silence,
Filling up the cave of my heart,
Veil upon veil, removed...
Taking a silent flight
within...

The language of imagination is symbols.

You may have to rely on your intuition to decode symbols. This may be an intimidating proposition but please know you have a better understanding of symbols than you are aware of.

Try this: Look at a person that fascinates you and imagine what type of animal that person could be. What type of tree would that person be, what type of flower? What type of music would this person be? What kind of geometric symbol would I assign to this person?

What kind of color would I assign to this person?

Now close your eyes and ask your intuitive intelligence what animal you would be, what color best describes you, what geometrical symbol would you attribute to your essence? Once the symbol shapes up, look for it in other places in the world.

Einstein used visualization techniques to arrive at some of his theories, including that of relativity. On that occasion he sat and imagined what the world would look like if you rode on a beam of light through the universe. He often used visualization techniques as his preferred method of discovery. Aside from using the parts of the brain involved in rationale thinking Einstein used imagination and order to get intuitive insights. He shunned traditional methods of discovery and encouraged everyone to open up to the infinite possibilities of the universe. Not being a proponent of traditional learning methods he utilized the creative side of his brain. He looked at things through different eyes to seek hidden solutions to problems at hand. He thought outside the box and allowed his intuition to bring to him solutions via the means and language of imagination.

Einstein was of the opinion: "We can't solve problems by using the same kind of thinking we used when we created them".

Can you recall a time when you asked and searched for a solution, kept it on your mind constantly and one day, suddenly, out of the blue, the answer came?

Intuition sky rockets when one focuses on a topic. We attract the answer after feverishly asking for it.

The price that needs to be first paid is a relentless, intense quest, day and night keeping this quest on your mind...

And then one day the pieces of the puzzle fall into place. Voila', the solution has arrived!

Passion is the currency, the needed investment before intuition shows the answer!!! Then we are in the natural flow and intuition tells us what we need to know when we need to know it.

Oftentimes imagination is the means through which intuition comes through. And the capacity to visualize concepts brings intuitive solutions into manifestations.

My father-n-law comes to mind when I think of a perfect example of how imagination inspired a creative solution. People who knew him described him as an over enthusiastic child with a loving heart. He was the kind of guy who identified the make and year of a car blocks away when he heard its roar down the road. He felt compelled to do this not to impress people but because he had to: he was a great car lover and loved all things technical as they related to cars. Needless to say he was a highly skilled Porsche and race car mechanic for an established racing team in the 60s. To me he illustrates how intense pondering on a solution coupled with a brilliant imagination lead to a needed discovery.

In 1970 he knew that the Porsche engines were running hot and he figured out the best way to remedy that was with a front oil cooler. At that time there was no oil cooler available so he went to Aircraft Aeroquip—a company that designed and built aircraft components- and he purchased an air plane oil cooler. He saw the cars were running hot and thought if a front oil cooler can cool the engine for a small airplane it could probably cool the engine of a race car. He held a ninth grade education from Germany, hardly spoke English and was not a well traveled man. What he had was sheer focus, self taught knowledge of cars, determination and a clear vision: to find a solution for overheating Porsches in the racing environment. He tweaked and installed it on a Porsche and built it into a 911 Porsche. This was never done before and he did this in 1972. Porsche eventually developed this cooling system on a larger scale.

So how did this simple man pull it off?

My father- in- law was often hunched over his drafting table figuring out the specific transmission ratios needed for each race track. My husband remembers his father pondering for hours over his own calculations, revising, testing upon installation and recalculating some more. Hours passed without him noticing. He was engulfed in this quest and it captivated his attention fully. In my opinion, intense pondering coupled with a vivid imagination fueled by a visible need brought into manifestation a great device.

The universe knows when we need to know what we need to know and provides us with that information in the most perfect of timing. And oftentimes, imagination is the bridge between your brain and God.

Chapter 4
EXPERIENCING INTUITION

Listen to your hunches: Heaven talks in snippets,
not in speeches...
Angels whisper fast...

Neale Donald Walsh

A friend of mine was getting ready to move to another town where her family lived and was worried about finding work there. She approached this search with a well thought out game plan: looked at employment ads, sent off resumes and went to a job fair. As she was going to her new gym in town, she sat next to a lady in the dressing room and chatted. Just when this lady was about to leave, her purse fell to the ground, opened up and out slipped her business card. My friend picked it up and gave it back to her and commented about how she would want to work for a company like hers. This triggered the spontaneous answer:"We are hiring, why don't you keep the card and give me a call".

And hired she was a short while later...

So was this just a coincidence that she found herself in that spa? At precisely the time when this other lady worked out? Or was my friend experiencing her own intuition in action?

How do we experience intuition?

It can come as a sudden surge of energy right before an idea or an image comes into our minds. Other times intuition comes softly and gently: like a whisper of a few words that bring an instant clarity to the matter at hand. Yet other times intuition comes as flashes of images that provide a perspective which in turn leads to a deeper understanding.

Not always do we receive intuitive messages all at once. We may feel we have just been given a profound message but may be at a loss as to understanding it in its entirety.

Daily, you and I may receive ideas, feelings, images that can be classified as intuition. We may not even notice these inflowing messages and yet they keep coming. These messages also come through your dreams. As intuition enters our system it affects our emotions, body and intellect. Let's look at how each level is affected by intuitive messages:

Body: we may feel an electric jolt, the hairs on the neck raise; a shiver of nervous energy in our gut, along our spine. Agitation, the urge to do something...

Emotions: we feel excited, we feel inspired, we are in shock!

Intellect: we instantly "know" something important and meaningful has registered; we now seek out more understanding by analyzing this newly received message...

These senses in combination can produce within us the urge to initiate a particular action.

So when are these manifestations in body, mind and emotions real and when are they repressed emotions, fantasies, non- processed stuff?

How can we separate true intuitive messages from memories, imagery of previous experiences, un examined data from our subconscious?

Quieting the mind is one way of letting pure intuition come through. Inviting an intuitive solution to a problem, challenge, a stumbling block, I call that pondering.

Symbols may carry messages that will need to be interpreted. As Carl Jung and others have shown, the unconscious mind often uses religious, mythological and occult symbols in dreams to get our attention. These symbols speak our cultural and social language. They have grown out of our own experiences and on an intuitive level we know what these symbols mean.

Best way to decode one's own symbology: become more self aware. Seek out silent moments, ask the question and allow time for the answer to come via different channels: the body, mind and emotions.

Psychometry may be another way of accessing knowledge about one object via intuition. Psychic feedback about a certain business opportunity becomes increasingly more sought after.

Another intuitive sense is Precognition; it means entering an intuitive state and being able to know ahead of time of an event as it will be played out.

People can have intuitive insights either through inner vision or through sensing. Inner visualization can be trained. By focusing inner attention totally on an object, by losing oneself in that focus on an object inner vision comes. By focusing on inner sensing, of feeling empathy deeply, one can channel intuitive messages also. Key is always the ability to keenly focus inner attention and that takes practice.

Two draw backs occur when it comes to intuitive insights: first, the ego can get in the way; thoughts can create a barrier interfering with the focusing of inner attention.

Secondly, inaccurate interpretation of an otherwise accurate experience can derail the understanding and the proper application of intuitive experience. Glamour and paranoia are also enemies of accessing intuitive insights.

When the ego gets in the way it comes from this left brain thinking that everything is either this or that. We are either right or else we are wrong. In our culture we staunchly defend facts, use facts to be made to appear right so looking towards intuitive knowing to grasp the essence of something is not so defendable. We discredit this intuitive knowing with the mind and by doing so, intuition is being shut off again. One can mature the logical mind and focus on maturing the intuitive mind. Together they can propel us unto a level of higher knowledge and knowing. From there wisdom gets accessed, divine knowing comes.

Wishing to develop a more in depth understanding of another person's psyche as is the case with a therapist/counselor or tapping into a state of mind that is separate from the thinking mind as may be the case with the creative process of an artist before the painting takes physical shape is wishing to move into an altered state that brings forth intuitive intelligence.

Preparing for intuition through the visual route takes emptying the mind. Focusing on a clean, empty slate...Irina Tweedie describes one technique I find visually fascinating: a picture within a picture: watch thoughts coming and going, fewer coming and going and see each thought slowly drowning. Floating above the lake, sinking into the water and drowning. Now the lake is serene, nothing to see but the serene, placid water, no ripples, no floating objects...Just a quiet surface...And from that quiet surface intuition arises and floats like mist over the lake...

So HOW do we get intuition to manifest?

Vision may be one way intuition manifests: dreams, imagination, visualizing, fantasy, a picture in mind's eye. Déjà vu experience of meeting some one that reminded you of someone, imagery, dream images that speak volumes...

I look at my daughter's art work and intuitively know her state of mind and emotions. Her art images tell me instantly where she is at...

Here's is how my own power of visualization helped me attain the kind of work I desired...

I always wanted to work in a hospital after finishing my graduate studies in clinical social work at Florida State University. I did not have a specific hospital in mind, just knew I wanted to work in a hospital. I remember working for a child development agency and found it did not meet my professional needs. Knowing that I needed to move on, and being the kind of person who always wants to attend yet another conference, I distinctly remember sitting in my car one day and pondering on how to persuade my current agency to give me time off from work to attend this social work conference in Ft. Lauderdale. I knew somehow this was an important conference...So I fought for time off and it was granted!

As I went from offering to offering, enjoying most of them, I settled into a presentation about visualization and relaxation (yet another strange coincidence, in retrospect?) For one specific exercise I was paired up with three other people. During break I chatted with some of them and to my surprise found out the lady in this group was from my home town and worked for a prominent hospital as a transplant social worker. I was immediately intrigued and wanted to know all about the kind of work she did. We parted by exchanging phone numbers and I heard her say:"Give me a call sometimes; we may need social workers in our department!"

I did follow up with her and was hired within months. The rest is history, they say...

My vision, my hope and dream was walked to the finish line by this little thing called intuition....

Another way of intuitive expression comes through hearing a **Voice:** you may hear a little voice telling you to either stay away from a person or to leave a certain situation. I heard the little voice in the "cab" on the way to my home town in Romania: it clearly told me what to say to keep me out of harm's way.

Sensation: Do you ever remember entering a house, a building and feeling a cold chill, a creepy feeling, a knot in your stomach, your heart racing and you feeling literally sick to your stomach?

One evening, leaving a grocery store chain and heading to my car I was approached by what looked like a homeless person, in tattered clothes, an old base ball cap pulled tightly over his eyes. He came towards me, one hand held out, his face slightly leaning to the side. I automatically grabbed my purse, opened it to look for cash.

The clasp of this particular purse jammed as I tried to open it in search for my wallet, so I wrestled with it, looked up and felt like making conversation while undoing the clasp. As I looked up while fiddling with my purse I saw a chilling sight: this guy's eyes were cold and piercing, he moved closer like a silent cat of pray and one of his arms lifted up. I froze and felt this sickening jolt to my stomach. I instantly knew I was not safe. I heard myself yelling: "Freeze, my brother has a gun while pointing at my car"!! He turned sideways, lowered his arm and disappeared between cars in the parking lot. I trembled, knees shaking and exhaled. Once in my car, safely locked in and engine going, I moved into traffic; I chuckled, shaking my head: I neither had a brother nor did I have a gun. As a matter of fact I did not believe in guns.

I guess this is yet another example of how intuition works: in the millisecond you enter a new room your brain analyses the input from all your thinking, the input from all five senses, and your entire lifetime of experience. Your whole brain immediately analyzes the situation, compares it to your life time of experience and gives you a "spontaneous" gut level feedback on the situation at hand. All this feedback occurs instantly and on a non rational level, and it gives you either a thumbs up feeling of safety or a sense of gloom and doom.

Yet another story illustrating a strange **sensation**, an anxious gut feeling comes from my friend Caroline. Here is her story:

While we were living in Hawaii many years ago- I am guessing it was about 1970, I got out of bed one day, the kids were already off to school and it was a beautiful and sunny day, beautiful clouds in the sky. We lived close to the mountains and when I got up this particular morning I felt very anxious.

I did not know what it was, I just had this weird feeling that something was wrong and I did not know what it was but I kept saying to my husband Dan: "something does not feel right!" I did not know what it was and I kept going to my solar plexus, I was really upset and I did not know what it was. I only knew something was wrong with my family. Well, this feeling of anxiety would not go away and I grew more and more anxious and finally I said to Dan, let's go take a drive. Dan worked nights at that time, and he was home during the day. So we took a ride and went up to this beautiful lookout and again, I became very anxious. Here I was on this awesome lookout, surrounded by blue sky and this incredible view and I could not breathe: I could not exhale, could not distract myself and could not get past how anxious I felt that day!!! So I said: "we need to go back home."

I felt something was wrong and I just knew I would get a phone call.

That was way before the time of computers and cell phones. Anyway, we went back home. Dan was not happy about this abrupt derailment of his plans and blamed it on menopause. But I knew better: I knew something awful was coming my way and I needed to be home by the phone.

At home, I sat, my stomach in knots, staring at the phone on the kitchen wall. As much as Dan wanted to distract me with a sweet gesture I told him: "Dan, stop it, this phone is going to ring…and it's not good news". Dan looked at me with dismay. And sure enough, the phone rang and it was my ex husband Greg. As soon as he said who he was I asked" what's wrong"? "What's wrong with Joe? (Joe being my younger brother). And Greg, my ex husband said to me: "Joe is dead. Joe is dead!"

I screamed and I guess I passed out and in the meantime Dan, not really knowing what we were talking about, hung up the phone. But when I finally got my senses back I made a phone call to my brother's house and yes, they confirmed, Joe just died in a car accident.

Intuitively, I knew there was something wrong with one of my family members and my intuitive gut sensation announced the news.

↬↫

7

Chapter 5
POWER OF PERSONAL WORLDVIEW

There are only two ways to live your life.
One is as though nothing is a miracle.
The other is as though everything is a miracle.

Albert Einstein

What tools do you bring to your intuitive process? Are you an optimist or a pessimist?

When working with the intuitive process, optimists usually aid the flow of information and energy. Pay attention to your level of negativity. Not all positivity is helpful, though. Forced constant positivity may cloud your level of realistic assessment of a situation and may ultimately block intuition. Without common sense intuition can be a loose cannon. We need to engage our own inner sense before we invite intuitive messages...like cleaning the house before the guest comes...

So are you willing to be innocent like a child again, look through the eyes of innocence, allowing your dreams to help you place one foot in front of the next?

Are you ready and capable of listening to the voice of your soul clad in the garment of a dream, vision, or a hunch?

Are you ready to align your energy field to be receptive to intuitive moments? After all, these moments do not arrive announced by trumpets; they come silently creeping into your energy field...

The guest arrives quietly when the door is open...Are you ready to welcome the guest?

How can you avoid common pitfalls?

As you become more prone to sensing intuitive moments you may ask yourself about how willing you are to trust these moments: to go down the wild river without a paddle and trust that it will transport you to the shore, are you ready to ask for guidance from your soul?

The mystery of life can be decoded through intuition. To give meaning to your life, existence has given you intuition. Are you ready for that? When you now live like life is a mystery, when you voice a wish, life responds: suddenly you find yourself getting your heart's desire after you casually put out your request. Key is for a clear message to go out and to be receptive for an answer to come in. For that you need to let go of control, to be neutral and receptive.

In order to tune up your intuitive powers use your body, allow your body to feel.

Each day as I drive to work in the morning, I relax in the car, empty my mind and invite intuition through a feeling, a gut hunch, a body sensation...I invite the guest to come by keeping my body alert and ready to register an intuitive message. I also keep a small recorder in my car in case images flow, insights come, etc.

Have a commitment with yourself to pay attention, to listen within, to feel and register. Your dreams may then hold the key to the mystery Einstein referred to...

An inadvertent talk with someone at the elevator door may lead to an opportunity, a meeting with your dream...Listening to someone's struggles and how they overcame the challenge may give you an intuitive clue for your own life.

When at home I often put pen to paper and allow direct writing to flow. No preconceived ideas, no goal, no outlines: just the flow of intuition through the pen to paper.

Intuition can come in illogical ways: I enjoy going to the library and letting my intuition guide me to a book on a shelf. Allowing that book to open where it needs to and the message may be in one of the lines...Or pulling out a music tape and allowing that particular melody to jumpstart the intuitive flow. In my opinion, music is particularly powerful...As I edit this document I listen to this hauntingly eerie chant by Jennifer Berezan called Returning. Olympia Dukakis, the well known American actress describes this as: "Motherheart whispering to us from over the ages, yearning for us to know her".

Sleeping in the rain is another of my favorite sleep time CDs.

I can only assume music has something to do with readying our energy fields for expansion to intuitive levels...

Your attitude and openness towards intuition will allow it to come to you time and time again. How you view the world will influence how you live your life. You get from the world what you expect off the world.

My friend Caroline panicked one day, called me for help and was a bit frazzled:"How am I going to move from the smaller condo to the larger this weekend? I have a bad back, don't know any guys who could move the heavier pieces of furniture and your husband is out of town". I quietly smiled and shook my head, thinking: "You do not trust the universe. No faith in getting help, Caroline". I assured her I would be over the next morning and told her not to worry: the move is on and it will get done. She was not very convinced but did not say so.

Next morning, coffee mug in hand, I headed over to her condo. She was already busy packing house hold items into big boxes and was glad to see me. I knew we would find help for the sofa and heavy pieces of furniture. Before she even realized it was time to consider moving the sofa I approached two young fellows in the parking lot, asked them for help and they moved the items. She had a look of disbelief and consternation on her face: I saw the question on her face. "How did you do this, are you sure you did not know, pay, plan for these two fellows to show up?"

I simply trusted the universe to provide; as a matter of fact I had the expectation that help will manifest and it did. It always has...

We need to be patient and allow intuition to unfold when a long term change in career is in the offing. Be patient and gather the pieces of the puzzle, and once put together the larger context is revealed.

Beware of what you focus on: if you keep an idea, a goal in focus daily and hope to find a solution be prepared to take in an answer: pondering is an underrated art. Then, suddenly, people call it "coincidence"....But then there is no such thing as a coincidence!!!

Why do you decide to take the scenic ride home versus your regular route via freeway? Just to discover you missed a four car pile-up...

Trust is nourishment for intuition. Fear shoos intuition away. Contracting through fear makes intuition an unwelcome guest. Trust throws the doors wide open. Self defeating, distrustful world views keep the guest out. They keep all positive life affirming manifestations out. Resisting the guest through fear and doubt shrinks your capacity to grow. It then becomes a self fulfilling prophecy: see, the world is a dangerous, hostile, scary place where no one steps in to help! Well, guess what: you create what you believe. You attract what you focus on. So be careful what you casually believe in, foster, nurture and subscribe to.

Remember you and YOU only chose your world view, your attitude, and your lens.

Doubt kills incoming help; it cancels out all possibilities for magic, it takes away the oxygen for intuition to breathe.

Should you always trust your gut? Always...

This is what Sandy knew; she knew that she knew: to AL-WAYS trust her intuition. Even if it meant inconveniencing a regular routine. By trusting her intuition she...

Well, let me let Sandy tell you her story:

Everyone has intuition to some degree. Some people listen to the messages they receive and others fight them. Intuition comes to different people in different ways. I think for most people it is a gut feeling. For some people it comes in the spoken word, for others it comes out of the blue, no consciousness about it, just a message arrives and they do not know where it came from. For other people intuition comes in form of visions, things they see with their own eyes. Other people receive intuitive messages through voices they hear in their head, not audible voices, just this little inaudible voice nudging...They just hear this little voice and they did not know where it came from. So, intuition comes in all different forms...

Intuition affects my life in lots of different ways and I have learned over the years to not try to logically think out where the intuition came from and to just follow the instinct and I found when I do that my intuition is always, always right.

The intellectual thought process may, however, not always be that way.

One of the most dramatic effects intuition has had on my life is how, by following my intuition, I was lead to save someone else's life.

This following story is about a young girl, 16 years old whose name I found out is Amber. Amber was in a very bad car accident. The day the accident happened I was in my place of business, a flower shop in Keystone, northern Florida, working and I was extremely busy. At that time I was dating a fellow, another business owner in town who wanted me to ride with him to Gainesville after work, after I closed up my business, to do some shopping. My initial instinct upon hearing his request was to say no, I am too busy and cannot leave my shop. My intuition however kicked in and I heard myself saying:" Fine, I will do this".

The plan was to meet him at his place of business under the condition that we will then go directly to Gainesville turn around and come right back because I was very, very, very busy and needed to go back to work to complete orders for the upcoming holiday. He agreed to those conditions so I left my store and headed to his place of business. As I walked into his store I noticed he was playing cards with one of his employees. They were not busy and he was not in a hurry to get in the car and leave. So I sat my purse down, waited for a few minutes and said to him:"Oh, are we going to Gainesville because I am really busy and do not have much time?" And Mike said:" Yes, we are going just as soon as we finish this game of cards. We are going soon, just wait a minute..."

I felt my emotions rising and I got very angry; I felt my original conditions were not heard and/ or were dismissed. I felt he did not appreciate that what I had going on was important. As I became more and more angry I decided that I was not going to wait for him, turned around and got ready to walk out. As I flung my purse over my shoulder and turned towards the door I suddenly got this distinct spike of intuition. I almost heard an audible voice in my head that said: "Be patient and wait because you need to go with him to Gainesville". Knowing that intuition is always correct, I said: "Oh, o.k." I decided to wait but did this grudgingly since I felt at this very moment I had many more things to do then go on this trip to Gainesville. So I turned around and waited. He brought his things, loaded them into his truck while I got more and more disgruntled.

But again my intuition was saying: "You need to do this; you need to go on this trip with him". As we approached a fork in the road where we needed to make a decision which road to take as they both lead into Gainesville, we discussed which way to go and decided to go left. As we turned left we suddenly saw this accident in front of us that blocked the road. I quickly took in the sight and again got this distinct message: "You need to remain here for the person who is in the back seat of this car."

Not knowing where this message was coming from, I was just following my gut. Before Mike was able to stop our truck, I felt the urge to get out and run towards the car. Mike was yelling:" Wait till I stop the truck, where are you going?" I looked around and said" I have to go help the person in the back seat of the car" not knowing why and what happened. As a matter of fact neither one of us knew who was in the back seat of the car since we just stopped our truck. I was shocked to hear myself say I needed to help the person in the back seat of the car. I ran out of the truck to the vehicle and to the back seat door. There I saw this teenage girl. I immediately noticed the greatest damage to this car was on the side where this teenage girl sat. As I opened the door and crawled in next to her I saw her being alert, she was talking, had her seat belt on and did not appear to have any physical damage to her body at all. I asked her if she was ok and before she could answer I got a very clear message to stay with her and to let no one move her until the ambulance arrived.

So I sat with her, held her hands and as she could feel my touch, I knew she felt comforted by it. We quietly sat waiting for the ambulance and the rescue squad to arrive.

While we waited, Amber's girlfriend who was with her in the car and was now standing outside, reached in through the back window and wanted to pull her out. Panic must have overcome her...I tried to talk her out of it, explaining Amber should not be moved and to please not pull on her. She stopped yanking at the door...

After about ten to fifteen minutes of waiting a woman in surgical scrubs approached the car, saying she was a nurse and wanted to precede getting Amber out of the car. So I quickly said:" No, we are not moving her, not until the rescue squad gets here".

So she walked away.

Another ten or so minutes later a man wearing a fire department t-shirt came up to the vehicle and said he needed to move her out of the car and I asked if he was with the rescue squad and he responded he was an off duty fire fighter. I said: "You are not moving her till the rescue squad gets here; she has got a back injury".

And he also moved away.

Looks like I kept fending off people and kept getting this enforced urgent message that she needed to be kept immobile until professionals arrived.

Finally, the ambulance arrived, approached the car and I told them this girl had a back injury and they went to get their equipment. I turned to Amber and told her:" I will now get out of the car since the rescue squad is here and ready to take you out of the car." She looked dazed and nodded her head. I assured her she would be ok. She did not want me to leave her, wanted me to stay right by her side, but the only way for the rescue squad to get in was for me to get out. They proceeded to enter the vehicle to move Amber out and I walked back to Mike's truck and we took off to Gainesville.

During the ride he asked me what all of this was all about? He apparently had never seen me involved in an unexpected event like this and shook his head…and I said I had this intuition, something speaking to me that I had to stay with that girl and that I knew she sustained a back injury, nothing visible and that I was told to remain with her in the car. That was sort of the end of the conversation.

Upon returning to my shop I told this story to several of my employees who were very busy but listened with interest. This girl's condition was very much on my mind and my heart and I was hoping to find out how she did.

The next day as I was talking with my employees a customer came in and I waited on her—this lady who came in wanted to buy flowers for this girl Amber. One of my employees who overheard the transaction came running back to me and said:" This is the girl's grandmother who was in the accident last night". I walked towards her and said:" Is she ok?" Her grandmother said:" No, she's got a severed spine and is in ICU in traction waiting for a surgeon who is qualified and experienced to stabilize her vertebrae so that her spinal cord would not be further injured. "

I nodded in shock…

She asked: "Were you there at the accident?"

I said "yes, I stayed with your granddaughter until the rescue squad arrived" and she exclaimed:

"O my God, you are the blond headed angel…!"

I said "What are you talking about?"

And her grandmother proceeded to say that Amber said there was a blond headed angel who sat in the back seat and held her hand. Amber was describing this person with blond curly hair. I said I was there but am not sure about her seeing an angel…

About two weeks later a blond woman came to my store and asked me what my name was and I answered my name was Sandy. She came around the counter and threw her arms around me, started crying and said:" I wanted to thank you for saving my Amber, I am her mother. The fact that you stopped, sat with her and kept everybody from moving her is the reason she is still alive today. They fused her spine and if she was moved she would have either been paralyzed or a paraplegic at best. Your presence there, you being with her, caused her to be ok and alive. We are so grateful to you Sandy".

Taken aback by this emotional outburst I said: "It was not me, I was just listening to some voice from God or the angels and did what I was told to do. I only listened and followed instructions, adding": I am so glad Amber is ok".

Yet another few months later I got to meet Amber in person again. I received an order for a flower arrangement and since my regular delivery person was not in that day I decided to make the delivery myself. As I arrived at the house the door opened and Amber's mom was saying:"Oh, it's you, you gotta come in and see Amber!"

I went in and met this beautiful young teenager about to graduate from high school. She was walking and talking and was doing so well. Amber was so grateful to me and I told her I was just listening and did what I was told to do.

This was a wonderful event, and again I realized how important it was to yet again listen to my intuition and do what I was told.

So having heard this testimony of trust in intuition, how do YOU make the shift from fear and doubt to love and trust?

It takes effort to pay attention to your moment to moment state of mind: what do you think now? How does that thought make you feel, what kind of side thoughts does it produce? What happens when you shine the light of awareness unto the NOW?

I personally find once I do pay attention to my thoughts and feelings that my rambling routine thoughts fizzle out and when I invite positive, trusting and life affirming views, the negative, angry thoughts die out. I guess it's the concept of weeds crowding out the flowers...or flowers crowding out the weeds...

Broadening your world view, deepening your trust, aligning your personality with your Higher Self, your soul, will keep you open to intuition. We are so used to doing, running, having, running and doing some more that stopping to not do, to not run, to not have, to not think is a scary proposition like watching ourselves fall into a void. And yet, when we slow down the doing, thinking, and running we briefly hover in the void, that meditative space of NOW and reconnect with our soul. The personality rests and the soul IS! When we stop thinking, doing and running we get a chance to experience BEING!

Being recharges your batteries, your creative energies flow, this opens the channel for intuition to flow again and then we become inspired with a new vision for creating. In that gap, when you allow yourself to be, you are instantly in touch with your soul's wisdom. Going from being to thinking to doing to being then thinking and doing is a rhythmic thing, the law of Rhythm in full manifestation. Natural flow happens in this rhythm.

Your brain and body takes time to interpret and manifest the wisdom of your soul. The soul, however, is always ready to share its wisdom with you...knows everything at once but your physical vehicles take time to interpret, analyze, and gain impetus to bring into the physical realm the inspiration received from the soul via your intuition. Allow yourself time between being and doing and being again and do not overtax your system. When you do, over expect and push, no one seems to see or hear you, you are overwhelmed, have no confidence, your mind is fuzzy, you become compulsive, feel desperate. You run out of motivation and life is stuck.

Pausing to shift into Beingness then looks like the biggest defeat. At that point we tend to want to run faster, try harder, pull harder as long as nobody stops us and has us feeling the NOW.

When we finally stop we are burnt out, our world view is defined by anger, distrust, fear, scarcity and no possibilities. And yet, breathing, closing your eyes, falling into that gap, feeling your body's fill with the prana of deep breath, relaxation, thoughts drowning one by one, hectic thinking gone, you surrender and allow yourself to drift in the sky the way white clouds do...

Now your soul can reach you, fill your body with energy, your mind clears off the cobwebs, and you are back in the natural flow. This is the time to pay attention to your intuition.

Here is how you test this phase:
Look at ideas coming into your mind; visualize yourself doing it.

Which activity makes you feel good? Which involves too much will power and effort? Which idea frightens and irritates you?

Then look at the actual activities you are still involved on a daily basis: are they filling you with enthusiasm, joy, excitement and creative juices? Close your eyes and allow to feel the response to each question: go into the gap, breathe and let go.

Then look at the answer to each activity: check in with your feelings,—the thermometer to how well your life flows: this one feels dead, this one excites me and feels meaningful, this one feels heavy and rusty..

Then ask for intuition to tell you which activity should be let go of: there is a season for everything; trust in endings so that you can trust in beginnings. Beginnings and endings, the law of Rhythm at work...

A time to live and a time to die...the law of Rhythm in action. If you hear yourself say "I should do this", please know the Should is the obstacle. If you hear yourself say: I Love doing this, the Love is the answer.

Whatever action gets the green light, feels right, is the one you need to do more of. See this new inspired action in your mind's eye, feel it developing, once you have a clear vision of it, energize it into creation by focusing on it with your senses, fill it up with your energy. Let your vision take clear shape in your mind and only then is it time for manifestation.

Start manifesting when the vision is ripe, not before. Allow the gestation to be complete before you step into the action of manifesting. And trust that your instinct will know when that time is.

Attitude is everything: Most people do everything to not face their dark sides; they label their state of being: joyful, moment by moment, in bliss.

In actuality they want to rush as quickly as possible through the dark tunnel of growth to the light and no matter the source of this light (It may be the light of an oncoming train...?) let's get through this as fast as possible so that we can rest again in one's own known comfort zone (or oblivion).

So how do you notice hypocrisy and ambiguity in your intuitional quest?

You do this by closely paying attention to your observations of hypocrisy and ambiguity in others. What you notice in others is a direct reflection of what you have within you. In order to test this premise list five things that offend you and get you mad: as you note the kinds of behaviors that upset you, what do YOU want to tell the ones displaying that behavior? Might you be guilty of the same behavior?

Gossip is such a powerful deterrent on our spiritual path: it gives one an immediate and very shallow satisfaction and leaves us feeling empty and disconnected in the long run. Be aware of your relationships based solely on negative and critical comments about others and gossip. How can one enhance trust and love on the murky waters of gossip?

Are you too greedy and ambitious in evaluating your own growth and that of others? Are you using your spiritual insights to impress others and to make them feel inferior?

Are you rigidly adhering to a very narrow way of perceiving things and excluding all other possibilities? This can slow your spiritual growth, impede your intuitive intelligence and keep you trapped in self importance and linear operating.

On the most well intentioned path to growing self awareness one can stumble on self importance, getting too bogged down with belly button analysis and miss the greater natural flow of intuitive knowing.

Every time you engage in extreme spiritual pursuits, take workshop after workshop, follow every spiritual practice that comes your way you lose yourself to the minutiae of technique. You will not have time or the need to focus on observing your own emotional feedback to pursuing intuitive intelligence.

୧୭ ୬ଟ

Chapter 6

TESTING AND TRUSTING YOUR INTUITION

We are here for fun;
We are here for learning;
We are here for remembering
Who we are...
And who we are...
The essence,
Always was, is and always will be.

Richard Bach

Philosophers, theologians, mystics, artists, poets, scientists, inventors and entrepreneurs all have used intuitive insights to be creative. So, can you trust your intuition? Should you trust your intuition?

How does one rely on this seemingly ephemeral guidance from beyond?

Here is how I put my intuition to the test...

It was the summer of 1988. I just moved to Florida from San Diego, after having obtained my license as a massage therapist, decided to open my own studio and was looking for a space to rent. I did not know where and how I would find it but knew beyond the shadow of a doubt that I would be led to it.

I was not going to look at the for rent column in the local newspaper, that much I knew. So I prayed and one evening I decided to get in the car and drive around town. As I sat behind the wheel I took a few deep breaths and went to a place of deep silence. There I asked for guidance...To please guide my car to the place I needed to find. To please get out of my own way and allow this guidance to come through. To please show me the way, literally.

I drove slowly and each time I came to an intersection I took time to feel which way I needed to turn. Was I meant to turn right or turn left? Each time I made the decision and kept driving. Suddenly I found myself pulling into a side street off the main road. Before I knew what I was doing, I saw myself pulling into this driveway, looked up and saw the words FCI on the building. Fitness Concepts Incorporated. And a phone number below it. I wrote down the phone number and drove home. I knew I found the place but had no inkling what made me so sure.

Next morning I called. The manager of the fitness center, Tom, answered the phone and I asked him if there was a space available for me to rent for my massage studio? He paused for a while and with a puzzled undertone in his voice asked: "Did Dave talk to you about wanting to advertise this space?"

"No", I replied. I did not know a Dave nor did I talk to anyone about an ad.

Again, he paused and explained:

" We are getting ready to place an ad in the newspaper about renting a space at our center, so please come in and let's talk".

When I met Tom later on that day, he again asked me how I knew to call him about this space:"Are you sure you did I not talk with Dave about this space?"

Yet again, I assured him, I did not know a Dave and went on to casually explain, I was just in the neighborhood and wanted to inquire...

Next day, after taking a tour of the place I signed a leasing contract for my massage studio. And Tom never found out how I was led to his place of business...

I guess, in those days I thought of this intuitive guidance as "spooky"...

Yet another intuitive manifestation was directly linked to this place called FCI; I must have needed this karmic connection to manifest an important relationship...

While at FCI operating my own massage studio I met Hans, a regular fitness member, who was then employed by a telephone company across the street and came in for work outs 2-3 times a week. He was shy, pleasant and we started talking. At that time I had no interest in dating anyone, was very happy with my life as a single and now successful entrepreneur and was slightly annoyed about his pursuit of me. After a few months of casually talking to me I agreed to go out to lunch with him. I remember sketchily talking about Europe, since he was born there, and about cars and places to see in Germany.

As I returned to work, I "knew" this: in my mind's eye a banner appeared, like an advertisement or a freeway traffic update: "This is your husband". As much as I wanted to shake off this image, it kept remaining there. The message was received.

We have just celebrated our twentieth wedding anniversary.

Karma being played out via intuitive intelligence!!!

৵৶

Chapter 7

DREAM MESSAGES

"The breeze at dawn
Has secrets to tell you;
Don't go back to sleep.
You must ask for what you really want;
Don't go back to sleep.
People are going back and forth across the doorsill
Where the two worlds touch.
The door is round and open.
Don't go back to sleep."
Rumi

Our intuition blossoms when we pay attention to our dreams, to our hunches, to these moments of heightened awareness when we KNOW something without the shadow of a doubt. Our job is to keep the house cleaned for the guest to arrive...keep the door open, keep the light on, pay attention to our dreams, listen to the small voice within, and validate that serendipitous encounter with a "stranger". Intuition needs our innocence, the clean and childlike way of seeing the world. The moments of unscripted delight, like a child discovering the pleasures of jumping into a puddle of water after the rain....

Every night as you fall asleep, you experience the pinnacle of your intuitive senses. At this time your brain waves slow down to 4-7 cycles per second and your capacity for relaxation, for healing, creativity and intuition increases by leaps and bounds.

Here are brain waves and their associations to daily activities and states:

In the BETA state- our normal waking conscious state- your brain wave frequency is between 14 to 33 cycles per second; this state is associated with the waking state where your five senses are fully aware, where you have a clear perception of time and space.

While in a light sleep you are moving into an ALPHA state with 7-14 cycles per second; this state is associated with the state of meditation and intuition. In the alpha state there are no time or space limitations.

When you reach the THETA state your brain wave frequency will be around 4-7 cycles per second and during this phase you go deeper and deeper into meditation, into that intuitive space.

In the DELTA state you are in deep sleep, it is a dreamless sleep, almost unconscious, with your brain wave frequency between 0.5-4 cycles per second.

The ALPHA, THETA and DELTA states are altered states of progressively deeper relaxation that are reached via meditation, hypnosis and deep sleep.

Intuitive messages come through many different types of dreams: creative dreams, precognitive dreams problem solving dreams, assuring dreams...

Following is a precognitive dream my friend Alisa had a few years ago:

.... I think it was early June, 2007. It was a dream about a friend of ours, Herb, who was in the hospital. It was quite a vivid dream. In this dream I see him in the hospital hooked up to all kinds of machines, breathing machines and in my dream I see one person standing next to Herb, patting him on the head and talking to him, and telling him "you will be ok", and touching his forehead and trying to comfort him. Looks like Herb is out of it, comatose by now, so in the dream that is all that I really see.

So next morning, when I wake up, it is Monday morning, I tell my husband: "Phillip, I had a dream last night about Herb and he told me he is going to die".

And Phillip says: "No, don't say that! He is not going to die; he has lots to live for!"

I said:"Phillip, stop!" I put my hand up "stop! Phillip, do you want to hear this dream or not? This is my dream!"

He did not want to hear what I had to say. But I felt compelled to repeat it:"It's a dream, Phillip. And in this dream Herb told me he is going to die. And there was a man in the room. And the man was petting him on the head and was talking to him, trying to comfort him. And then I woke up".

Of course Phillip wanted to hear none of it, and kept repeating:"Well, he is not going to die. But you know I went to visit him and managed to get into his room saying I was family. So you seeing this man next to Herb by his bed, that was me ".

"That really was me. I was in that room. "Phillip proudly announced.

Now I am puzzled.

"Phillip, how were you able to be by his side in the hospital room; he was not allowed to have any visitors, remember?"

Phillip went on:"A few days ago I went to the hospital to visit his wife Laura and quite a few family members sat out in the waiting room and every half hour or so someone would go in to say hi to him and come back out. Two nights ago when I again arrived at the hospital, the nurses told me the family had gone out to dinner. Then one of the nurses asked: Are you uncle so and so? And I said yes."

So Phillip was ushered into Herb's room and sat down next to Herb, petting him on the head, comforting him. He left after a while and the family was still not back.

By Wednesday morning I have another dream. In this dream I am sitting in the room with Herb, cross legged, Indian style at the foot of his bed and he and I are conversing, not with words but in spirit. Herb is saying to me:"It's ok; I don't want to live the way I would have to live ". These were his exact words. I took that to mean: he was not willing to do all the things he would have to do to recover given his weak heart, just to remain alive.

I guess this was the message Herb gave me for his family.

So again, the following Wednesday morning I told Phillip I had a dream. Phillip is getting ready to walk to the kitchen to make coffee and as he walks, he immediately snaps back:"No he is not, he will not die". So I remind him this is what I have dreamed.

"Phillip, listen to my dream, Herb is going to die, and he told me he wants to die and that is ok. He has already been in the spirit world and knows it is ok. "

And yet again, Phillip cannot accept this.

On Saturday, June 14, we received a call from one of the brothers in the brotherhood that Herb has passed away this morning. So why did Herb of all people come to me? I don't ever recall having had a conversation with him about life and death, nothing spiritual was ever discussed. We never talked about reincarnation; we never talked about anything like that. And yet he came to me and told me about his impending death. I guess his soul felt safe to tell me that he is going to die.

A year after Herb's passing they had the unveiling of his stone at the cemetery. Phillip and I attend the ceremony, people are grieving, crying, and it feels like we are burying him all over again. His daughter was there and we stepped out and I said to her:"At some point I'd like to tell you something your father told me before he died".

Weeks later I got a call from her and we met. She listened attentively and then said with a light smile around her lips: "I am so glad you told me about your dream; my dad did not want to go to endless rehab and I guess he decided it was time to go. This dream was a way for him to reassure me that the time was right..."

Intuitive dreams full of symbols are always about a process you are currently working on. Pay attention to themes repeated in subsequent dreams. Reoccurring dreams are especially important as they contain messages that you need to receive. They repeatedly drive the point home and demand your attention until an understanding is reached.

Here is one such reoccurring dream:

I have been dreaming for months now about being in a building to which I had no key or the windows and doors of the building could not be locked from the inside. Repeatedly, I would go through great efforts trying to lock the doors, trying to secure the window locks, trying to block entrance by barricading the door. Inadvertently it was always a preparation to settle in for the night and the feeling of lack of security pervaded all of those dreams. No matter how hard I tried, how desperate I was to make the room I found myself in secure, I would discover how easily the door came unlocked, time and time again. At one point I even made a mental note to bring a hammer and nails when traveling to new places (I guess there is humor even in dreams...).

These dreams repeated over months during the time I started working on this book. I saw myself in various beautiful houses, some moody Victorian homes with intricate wood work, others with light and airy rooms. The most recent dream of this kind was the last one that ultimately unlocked the message they all were meant to convey.

I was driving up the house in the mountains of North Carolina, walked up to the side of the house on the steep hill and as I approached the side yard I looked up and to my amazement saw another house sitting to the side partially covered by branches of a shade tree. I remember feeling surprised by this and as though I just remembered, I said to myself:"O, I guess this large house came with the property, how interesting, this is my house too. Let's check it out".

Approaching the back door I knew the door was unlocked. This gave me a moment of apprehension, not panic, just apprehension. And sure enough it was unlocked. Entering through this massive, dark wooden door, I found myself in the most magnificent, Victorian home, albeit a bit gloomy. Large floor to ceiling windows were covered with ornate window coverings, a coffered ceiling, decorative rail work. I walked from room to room thinking how interesting to discover all this and felt excited as I pondered how I could brighten it up and de clutter it.

Just then, from a side door come in children, helping themselves to apples on a tray on a side wall buffet. They acted like they have been here before, came to play, visit and were happy to be there. And after a while they left. And to my surprise nothing was destroyed, damaged or ruined. I looked around and remembered thinking:"Well, I am glad the doors were unlocked, new friends can come and go..."

For the first time these unlocked doors made sense.

And since then I felt light and at ease.

As I pondered the repeated theme in these dreams I saw a gradual decrease in fear of being in an unlocked house...This last dream certainly was a pleasant surprise: instead of fear I welcomed the open house.

So what did these dreams try to convey?

Working on this book made me discover how vulnerable I would become by putting my own very intimate thoughts and feelings out there by writing them down. I have never much talked about my own personal beliefs let alone shared intimate snap shots about them. And now that I write about them, to my surprise, I gain trust and feel this sharing is ok.

If we pause long enough to hear it, our intuition will speak to us through our dreams. So how do we go about inviting the guest to come through a dream? How best to go about recalling and remembering a dream?

Here are a few suggestions:

RECALLING A DREAM:
- Keep a notebook besides your bed; record your dreams as soon as possible after waking up

- Before falling asleep, request that your Higher Self remember the dreams you had and to let you recall them easily upon awakening
- If you wake up during the night, write down the entire dream with symbols
- Self suggest prior to falling asleep that you will be given a message in your dream to a problem you need a solution
- Immediately review your dream in the morning: look for the setting, the people in it, the action, the color, the feeling and the words
- Make an effort to review, analyze and extract meaning from your dream each and every time you have a vivid dream that appears to have a meaning and a message.

If dreams appear illogical there is the possibility you may have recalled only fragments of that dream. Another possibility is that this dream represents something illogical in the dreamer's life. Or else your own mental blocks have restricted your total recall of the entire dream.

If you cannot decode an important dream, suggest to yourself before falling asleep that the meaning be revealed in another dream. Dreams that remain unchanged through the years indicate the dreamer's resistance to change. Dreams of illness can be either literal or symbolic warnings.

When facing a problem for which you seek a solution, ask for guidance in a dream. Frame your question in detail, and ask that a solution come to you through a dream. Do this before you go to sleep. Be ready to record the coming dream in all its details.

And approach interpreting a dream by being practical: look for the obvious meaning first, and if the literal meaning does not make sense look for symbols that make sense to you. If in your dream you receive an unusual message reduce it to the symbols you use in your everyday life. Dreams come through with messages you are meant to get!

Carefully observe repeat dreams: they are an indication of a pertinent theme being repeatedly addressed from different angles.

Oftentimes, our dreams show us the way out of a dilemma; they are the response of our soul to daytime activities and challenges.

I believe dreams are not here to amuse us; they are here to guide and help us. They direct our attention to mistakes and offer direction and encouragement for solutions.

Do not fear conversations with the dead in your dreams; if the communication is one sided it signifies telepathy.

If both parties participate it signifies that this actual encounter has taken place on the astral plane.

Dreams are mostly guides to the development of one's life's purpose. They assist the higher self while in this physical body.

Dream symbols are the forgotten language of your soul: apply patience and diligence in decoding the symbols and applying the message to your everyday life.

When you have just "gotten" the meaning, when you have just decoded the message of a repeat dream, express your gratitude; the guest will come again and again when welcomed and appreciated!

Look for past life experiences in your dreams. These experiences appear not only in color but also with a certain appearance and setting in a certain time period. They are also designed to ease your confusion and to better help you understand this life's purpose. These dreams come to warn you against repeating the same mistakes, to explain your current relationships from a reincarnation standpoint and often times explain your reaction to people, places and environments.

Years ago I had such a dream.

…..For years as a young adult I had this great fear of dogs: all kinds of dogs, all sizes and breeds scared me. Walking on the beach, be it in Southern California or Florida, where beautiful golden retrievers and black labs frolic in the waves, tales wagging, wanting to make friends and seeing them run towards me would terrify me.

Every time a dog came running in my direction I would freeze and panic. No matter how illogical the reaction was and how often I told myself these are friendly creatures who just want to play, I could simply not shake this terrorizing and paralyzing fear. I remember trying to explain this terror by having been bitten by my own dog around age four or five.

Our mutt Nellie, squatty but fast at the same time, chased after me as I was running home from a neighbor's house, caught up with me and play bit me in my arm. I still remember feeling the terror of seeing this dog catch up with me, me falling and the teeth of Nellie showing. How could this one time "encounter" with my family dog create such a deep seated terror? Did this experience truly create the terror or did it reactivate an old existing terror?

In order to get to the bottom of this I asked to have the root of this terror revealed to me in a dream. And this is what the dream showed: I saw a gloomy street, and found myself approaching what looked like a huge pile of something along a stone wall. It looked like the dark ages, dogs and cats, all dead were on this pile and I saw myself as an old, weak, and dirty beggar, with brown, black rags, my head covered by a tattered hood, sitting by the side of the pile scouring for food. I am hungry and weak. As I turn around I see this big emaciated dog with crazed eyes, teeth flashing ready to attack. He pounced on me and all went black…I must have died…

I viewed all this with the detached perspective of an onlooker not the one that was just killed by a dog. As I woke up next morning I immediately "knew" this was the reality of what happened to me in a past life. Recognizing that broke the spell and allowed the healing process by slowly approaching puppies, then bigger dogs and gaining a sense of trust.

Does trauma always have to have roots in another lifetime? Not necessarily. It is certainly worth exploring, though…

Again, this chapter is not intended to provide an in depth explanation of dreams—there are many great books about dreams, symbols and interpretations available. This is meant to be only a reminder that there is so much learning and processing going on at the time when we sleep; in fact some of the greatest lessons are learned during sleep.

So how can one enter the halls of learning on purpose every night?

State your intention to your Higher Self before you fall asleep: I would like to gain insights into…or I would like to visit the library of ABC knowledge and come back with an understanding of xyz topic. If you seek a solution to a problem, ask that you be given access to this solution and ask that you bring this solution back in shape of a clear dream.

Do not sabotage this request by questioning your capabilities of "getting" the answer, remembering the dream and understanding its meaning. Keep an open mind, trusting that the answer will come.

When you wake up in the morning, linger a bit, let the dream remain in your memory a bit longer, feel the images you glimpsed, review them gently, and talk out what you see, what you feel, how this makes sense to you in the present tense. It is important that you feel you are IN the dream not looking back at it. I use a tape recorder and describe my dreams in detail each time. And if you are still not clear, ask again next evening to be shown yet again what you need to know. The more you validate this process of formulating a quest, asking, recording and interpreting your dreams the more you are programming your Higher Self to come through with answers.

In a way you ask to align your personality with your soul. And the soul never needs a break, does not need to sleep and is therefore always available for consultations.

⧟⧟

Chapter 8
SOUL MESSAGES

Soul: I came from brilliancy
And
Return to brilliancy,
And
While in this body
I grow, learn, suffer
And evolve...

Unknown

Intuition is linking us to the purpose of our soul, and once we are linked up to our soul we can never turn back. Living on the level of the personality with all its drama, fear and empty struggles for meaning will then come to an end. Once the personality submits to the guidance from the soul, life is lived with magical meaning. Intuition is that creative link to a place that has always been part of us, but mostly was only reached periodically and as a glimpse. We are born to create, to grow, to discover our own depths and heights, our own potential and intuition allows us to link up with those heights shrouded in the mists of the Himalayas. The Himalayas have always been here we just have not seen the solitary peaks, as they are covered in mist.

Intuition is the connection to those silent peaks within us, the watcher on the hill, the higher self wise beyond imagination...

Here is my own soul story...

1986—San Diego, California. I just started my first bartending job in Chula Vista—a dive in a blue collar neighborhood after purchasing my first car- a small white Honda I called Chiquita. Excited, I was embarking on this new adventure: single, renting an apartment overlooking Balboa Park, a few friends in town.

One afternoon, the juke box is playing, in comes a rugged looking guy, late twenties, dirty blond hair. He sits down and orders a beer. He takes little sips and looks around. The moment my eye caught his face- the first time- I couldn't stop looking at him. A strange feeling overcame me: "You are back, so good to see you. " No inkling as to why I felt this way, just could not stop feeling this way...Strange, how intuition works...

I went about my business but kept having this feeling each time he came in. Eventually, in his shy way, he asked me out. "What took you so long, my insides screamed?"

As I settled into the passenger seat of his car on the way to our first date at a restaurant I was shocked to find myself reaching over and resting my hand on his thigh. This was not typical of me, I knew. But I could not help it. The moment my hand touched the fabric of his shorts I felt like:"Finally, I get to feel you again, see you again, talk with you again". I must have mumbled a lame explanation or apologized, but Steve did not look a bit surprised. That was even more eerie. He and I talked, laughed, walked on the beach as though we have always known each other...

Later, in a psychic reading this was explained to me: In a past life during the cowboy days, Steve and I, both males, were best friends. I was a cowboy and Steve was the cook. He sustained an ankle injury and could not ride a horse well. But he could cook well. I in turn was an excellent rider. It so happened we were in love with the same lady we met at the saloon. We made a bet: whoever did a better job at the other guy's work will get the lady. So Steve (or whatever his name was then) swapped jobs with my male cowboy self for one entire week. Steve, with an injured ankle, apparently did poorly as a horseback riding cowboy. I, in turn, did well enough as a cook. On the last day of our bet Steve was thrown from the horse and trampled. As he lay dying, he whispered barely audibly: "The joke is on me" closed his eyes and was gone.

Now that I understand our past life together I understand why seeing him, feeling him, hearing him again was so exhilarating. I got a chance to have my old buddy back. I got a chance to live out unfinished karma...

And in real time in this incarnation, Steve turned out to be a great cook. He prepared great meals, served them with great attention to detail and he and I spent time enjoying each other's company.

Soul messages healing karmic ties...

Our souls bring in and manifest personalities, people and karmic ties in each incarnation to facilitate our healing...There is no such thing as nonsensical encounters; only misunderstood meetings with souls from another time. I have not seen Steve since then, almost three decades ago, and do not feel the need to reconnect. We found each other, met again in physical bodies and erased old karma. Do we need to meet again? I don't know and I am not worried. If the karmic need arises, my intuition will lead me to him...

More than dreams are taking place at night during your dreams; your higher self attends classes, joins other souls in learning and brings back the soul knowledge next morning.

My friend Alisa has noticed this dream based practice many a night...

When I first started to go to the Universal and Triumphant Church, the chelas there, they would say you would go to the Great Temples at night times and have dreams of wisdom. You would be in the Temples and see the Masters...While in the temples you would be taught on the inner planes and there would be times I would see people and I would recognize them and they would look very familiar to me. I would say: "you look so familiar to me, I am not sure where I know you from? "

And I would ask if they worked in a certain place and they would say: "No, we saw each other in the temple...

When I first heard that I did not understand what that meant. Over time I learned that at Temple we learn things, we get wisdom; we are members and attend the teachings in the Hall of Knowledge and bring back this knowing after we wake up in the morning.

These hook ups with nocturnal soul teachings may come in shape of angel connections, non incarnated guides and divine teachings. You and I may not know when we come back from the Halls of Learning, but we return with this unshakable sense of having been in the presence of the Divine.

Intuition is the gift of your soul to your personality to grow in this life time. You can never lose this gift although at times the gift is elusive; it comes unexpectedly and leaves suddenly. So how do you prepare for it? I liken it to a guest that has a standing invitation to visit. When a guest is expected one cleans the house, makes every effort to create an inviting, comfortable environment and then one waits: one KNOWS beyond a shadow of a doubt when the guest has arrived. And then one welcomes the guest...

When I welcome the guest I feel more alive, creatively juiced up, ready to push my known boundaries of what I held possible further out and discover gems and nuggets of gold strewn along the path. The manifested wisdom in the shape of insight comes from higher understanding, deeper trust in the Universe, a feeling of grace, a deep knowing of ancient knowledge directly dripping into my consciousness, bypassing the rationale mind, skirting by the emotional pond and reaching my Soul.

Intuition, the guest, brings the gift of knowing what you need to know when you need to know it.

When we share our intuition with others it is validated, becomes stronger, and our own truth is validated more powerfully, canceling out distrust, fear, doubt, limitations and old narrow ways of living life. With intuition one can yet again tap into miracles that were at our door step all along.

One of my intuitive moments came disguised as an out of body experience. I was at a retreat in the high desert of the Pacific Northwest, walking up to the house I lived in nestled among sage brush and juniper trees. As I climbed the steep mountain to the house, peace settled within me, I turned around and gazed over the opposite mountain ranges bathed in a warm golden Indian summer light. The house was cool and quiet. I decided to have a cup of herb tea and lay down on my bed. I must have dozed off since I immediately found "myself" hovering on the opposite wall atop the window covering. From there I looked down at my sleeping body on the bed. Fascinating! I thought. I was just laying down there and now I am up here looking at this familiar shape over there on the bed. I am not afraid to be up here, just a bit puzzled. So, does that mean I am not my body? Before I could wait for another insight I was right back on the bed, moving, waking up and looking at the window. I realized I was out of my body for a bit and this was ok. Not fear inducing, not freaking me out, just away from the body. And up to this point my head knew I was not the body but I never experienced it.

To experience it is to KNOW. And now I know beyond the shadow of a doubt. And death holds no more power...the myth is shattered, the truth was revealed!!!

Intuition is not the exquisite guest that comes to the few. We all can invite in this guest and what is most rewarding to know is this: the guest will come...It always comes when the house is quiet, the noise of daily living is removed and the space is prepared for the guest's arrival.

So how do you prepare the house for the guest bearing the gift of intuition? How do you welcome the guest?

Become quiet and centered. Allow all thoughts floating through your head to drawn in the water of your consciousness. Breathe and see the thoughts drown one after another till the surface of the stream is placid and still. Invite the soul into this picture. Allow your soul to breathe, sit there and be ready to receive intuition.

The intuitive intelligence uses input from your logical mind, your emotional body and connects you to your soul. This process can be called creativity, knowing or enlightenment. The mind is never the ultimate element in enlightenment; it is the stepping stone to be left behind.

Over the years my dance with intuition took on many shapes... So will yours. You never know how you will welcome the guest. But then who really needs to know. You cannot practice for the arrival of the guest; just get ready, be still, humble and silent and the guest will come....The guest always comes...

So why does one need to clean the house before one can invite intuition in? Junk impedes the flow, worries, information overload, hectic thinking, shallow breathing, being stuck in the head;—all impedes the entry for intuition.

Cleaning house means one is willing to switch to deeper breathing, going for a walk, allowing thoughts to come and go, not focusing on anything in particular.

Cleaning house means breathing in love, in trust, in awe of the blue sky and a pine tree swaying in the wind. The awe one feels when listening to the music in the pines. The awe one feels when one watches a white cloud floating in the sky...Nothing more to feel, just pure grace bowing down.....

Cleaning house also means looking into someone else's' eyes, smiling, and being honest in that gaze. Allowing the soul to come through your eyes.

Cleaning house means allowing a hug to touch your soul, to feel that heart beat with love and kindness.

The summer of 2009 when I drove across the magical mountains of Colorado and Wyoming with my teen daughter, I experienced awe and grace, -and the unexpected guest—just by allowing my heart to be open, to welcome the guest....

Your Higher Self constantly brings in wisdom to your personality from your soul. You may not hear a voice inside your brain, but what about a friend telling you something that hits home? How about getting a message from a stranger, or from a license plate, a bill board, a sign on a business door? What about cranking on the radio in your car and hearing a song's lyrics that speaks to you. Or cracking open a book and looking closely at the message it holds on that paragraph your eyes land on?

So how do you tune into the messages from your Higher Self, your Soul, God, the Angels, your spiritual guides?

Relax your body, focus on your rhythmic breathing, your heart beat, and listen within. Let all of your tension leave through the head, shoulders, finger tips, your belly, your buttocks, your legs, and feet...

Allow to note what you feel without labeling it; do not will anything, do not escape from what you feel. Allow the Flow of life to sweep through you and enjoy the vibration...

Silently feel gratitude for the vibrations inundating you, be still and feel...Welcome the guest! Allow, feel, breathe, feel gratitude and let it overflow the receptacle of your body...

Breathe and intonate the ancient Mantra of Unification:
The sons of men are one and I am one with them;
I seek to love not hate;
I seek to serve and not exact due service.
I seek to heal not hurt.
Let pain bring due reward of light and love.
Let the soul control the outer form,
And life and all events,
And bring to Light the happenings of the time.
Let vision come and insight.
Let the future stand revealed.

Let inner union demonstrate and outer cleavages be gone.
Let Love prevail. Let all men love.
A soul I walk on earth; I represent the One...
I am a soul and also love I am.
Above all else I am both will and fixed design...

Once you have established this soulful prayer with humility and openness, voice your need, be still and listen.

Then take the answer received and bring it into the physical: talk about it to a friend, discuss the dream and what your answer was with a friend, write it down, email it to yourself, and record it. Do all of it with gratitude, touch your heart and send gratitude upwards.

I had a dream just the other day and when I awoke I immediately knew it was an important dream. I found myself in a room with a quite well known person and was surprised; then I was ushered into another room that looked like an old fashioned school house and met the principal and the teacher there. I thought this was a meeting arranged for someone else to attend university there but was told no, you can sign up for a course here. I immediately thought I missed the deadline for this and was again told with a friendly warm tone: you are just in time to take a course. I looked around and saw an old antique desk, dark, worn floor boards and shutters in front of the windows. On the table was a model of the various academies on the campus. It felt like being in an old school house or a historic home at another time and another place.

When I woke up I knew I attended the halls of Higher Learning, I was given the knowledge I needed and it was just the right time for this knowledge to be delivered to me.

At night, after we fall asleep, we can go to higher realms and be given knowledge. We return the next morning to our sleeping bodies, having studied and come back with another deeper layer of knowledge, wisdom and understanding.

Sometimes one needs to shift from doing one thing to shifting into doing something totally different. When I sit at my laptop too long, and feel I am out of the natural flow I get up and walk around my back yard, look at the sky, listen to the birds, follow the trail of geese overhead to the neighboring pond.

Then I ask: What do I need to know now?

And keep walking without a specific aim, no demanding thoughts, just walking and gazing at the rose garden, the bees in the palm trees.

Chapter 9

INTUITION APPLIED TO EVERYDAY LIFE

Your soul, your spirit is crying for God
But God lives within you.
God is not in the books,
He is not in any teachings,
Not in the churches, not in the synagogues.
The answer is within you.
God is deep within the chambers of your heart.

Alisa Pearl

The message is clear when one listens...

Alisa's next story is very compelling:

It was June 11, 2004, a Friday and I went to Paula's house. I normally clean Paula's house on a Wednesday and by way of routine I would always leave my cell phone on the counter. But for some reason that day I took my cell phone and put it in my apron pocket. That morning was the memorial service of President Reagan some place in California. I rarely turn the TV on and yet that day I did. As I was cleaning the bedroom, beautiful music was playing, so beautiful and inspiring, I heard a voice saying:"Sit down, sit down."

Let me explain: I get messages by hearing them; I hear voices all the time. So I was not greatly surprised to hear: "Sit, sit down."

First, I wanted to argue with this, no, I don't have time to sit down. I don't have time to sit and watch the memorial service. But I finally gave in and I sat down anyway. No sooner did I sit down my cell phone was ringing and it was my grandson Jessie, 14 years old:

"Grandma, grandma, something has happened to Luke!"

"What, what? Tell me what's wrong?"

"I don't know, grandma, "

"Jessie, tell me what's happening with Luke, you have to tell me!

"No grandma, I don't know, I think he is in the hospital, I don't know what's wrong, though".

"Ok, I am coming right away. "

I sat on that sofa and felt a quivering through my whole body. It felt like my body was exploding from the inside, from my head to my toes. This quivering inside I could not explain at the time. I now know that that was the connection to my grandson Luke, who just died. My intuition brought this to my attention in form of this quivering.

Luke was a troubled kid, lonely and secretive. He hung himself from a tree. At the moment of quivering I did not know and yet I did know what it was.

I called Paula and explained I needed to go, something has happened to my grandson. I kept apologizing for leaving the house a mess. So I picked up my cell phone—why did I have my cell phone with me that day? God knew I was getting a call and had to have it on me that day. So I picked up my phone and drove to the hospital but decided to stop at Luke's house where police was gathering. I asked one of the officers:

"I don't understand this, what happened".

The officer turned to me and said

" He is ok now".

At first I did not understand but then I did on a soul level. Luke was ok now. Inside me I screamed: "God, don't let it be! Don't let it be" but I knew my grandson was gone. While driving to Shands Hospital I am screaming out to God: "help me, help me, and give me strength and courage. I need strength and courage. Not for me, not for me but for them, for everybody else, I need it for them, I need it for them!"

Even before I got there I knew Luke was dead. I knew he was gone; he was dead, even though I don't believe in death. Next thing I see myself calling Paula and telling her:

"Luke is dead; my grandson is dead. I am sorry I did not finish cleaning your house!"

Paula assured me she would take care of it and added: "just go and take care of your family."

So I went to the house and all the cop cars were around as I pull in the driveway. Are you the grandma? Before I could answer I heard myself asking "Is he?" and then my knees buckled. I did not go down, did not fall down, caught myself and stood up. I asked for strength and courage and I got it.

By time I got to the house my daughter was there. She said:"Mom, he is gone..." I said:"I know, I know..." And then she started to tell me what had happened.

His brother Jessie's girlfriend had a conversation with Luke and Luke wanted to ask that girl to be his girl friend. They were already friends, hanging out together. So this was the day he wanted to ask her to be boyfriend and girlfriend so he went to her house and asked her to be his girlfriend. She obviously turned him down and said:"Let's just be friends, not girlfriend and boyfriend". I believe Luke could not take another rejection, not one more rejection. As much as I told him I loved him, as much his mother told him, he never felt loved. At the moment Luke's soul ascended- I felt that, I understood that later. As he was moving out of his body something was moving out of me at the same time. I knew the moment when he was taking his last breath. So why did I feel it; why me? We did have a loving connection, a soul to spirit connection back to the source that I call God.

Another moment of intuitive premonition comes to Alisa's mind. Here's another of her stories...:

Phillip has this 89 year old friend Harold who with his wife Stella attend synagogue with us. Phillip and Harold belong to the Elder Brother Group and on occasion put together a luncheon where the elders meet. This one occasion came near and Phillip insisted he wanted to ride with Harold to the store to get the needed food and utensils for that gathering. I started having this gnawing feeling of doom about Phil riding with Harold and asked Phillip to consider riding with me instead. He vehemently disagreed with me saying he wants to go to the store with Harold. And the more he insisted the more I became determined to arrange my schedule to have Phil ride with me that Thursday. He finally was convinced and off we went to the store. We started purchasing the stuff and brought it to the synagogue next day.

Typically, Harold and Stella are always arriving early for these occasions to help us set up the tables, etc. On that day I said to our cantor Margaret:"I don't know what is happening, Harold and Stella are always early and today they are not here?"

Just as I was getting ready, key in hand to leave the building to get into my car and to look for them I hear cantor Margaret talk into her cell phone: "Calm down, are you ok? You got into an accident, Stella"?

And sure enough, Harold missed the usual exit to the synagogue and made an illegal u-turn getting hit from behind by another car.

I am glad I listened to my intuitive feeling gnawing at me and I am glad I acted upon it by changing my schedule and by driving my husband myself...

ॐॐ

Chapter 10

DEEPENING INTUITION AND CREATIVITY

Only as high as I reach
Can I go.
Only as far as I seek,
Can I grow,
Only as high as I look,
Can I see.
And only as clearly as I dream,
Can I be

So how does one deepen one's intuitive intelligence? How does one facilitate creativity based on one's intuition?

We talked about self awareness and that includes emotional awareness: an intuitive spark may create a positive, pleasant feeling in us and we feel joy and confidence in approaching action. It can also manifest strong feelings of sadness, fear, and we are propelled to kick into immediate action, and sometimes this looks like a heroic act, saving others, saving ourselves without any pre conceived action plan, just pure intuitive action jolt.

At times we feel inspired and do not know how to put that inspiration into action. Or we do not trust that inspiration enough to bring it out of the closet into the light of day.

I ask for divine guidance and request divine wisdom to show me the way to manifest this inspiration.

It takes cultivating hope and faith. Trusting the divine manifestations in our lives that help us on the path to this place in consciousness, to this very moment, to NOW.

Children have this wonderful ability to access intuition; they do not need to be reminded that life is a joyous expression in spacetime. And then as we grow up, we forget, we burry this intuitive wisdom under linear thinking, sarcasm, lies.

So how do we remember to remember?

This is a slow process of daring to allow a flicker of memory come into our focus: remembering a sight, a smell, a person whom we just met. A déjà vu kind of experience when deep down we know that we have met this stranger before. Then synchronicity happens: what one focuses on in thought manifests as experience: to the outsider it may look like a strange thing but we understand the meaning. We are being led towards what we need and what we love. That's how we find our passion.

Jonas Salk, the biomedical inventor of the polio vaccine invited intuition like a guest bearing gifts:"I wonder what my intuition will toss up to me like gifts from the sea".

"Intuition will tell the thinking mind where to look next".

So key then is to integrate the knowledge of the thinking mind with the wisdom of the intuitive mind and allow a quantum leap forward. An idea is born of the logical mind, gets thrown against the intuitional mind during pondering and out comes a new product: an inspiration for a brand new concept.

The drawback of the intuitional mind is inadequacy with words; the adequate verbal expression of a feeling, insight and a knowing usually falls short.

The intuitive mind best operates with succinct verbiage: frame a question, a quest for a solution in succinct language. Get to the core of the issue and use one succinct sentence. Nourish your intuitive intelligence by feeding it positive affirmations like:"My intuition will bring up the best answer to my problem". "I trust my intuition and listen to it".

Do decipher the picture, the metaphor, the symbol that comes we need to again listen to that uncanny jolt that says:"this is the picture you need to decipher".

By way of amplification, one associates many different meanings to one symbol. When that one picture reverberates within oneself then that is the picture one needs to decode.

Then incubate the picture; let it be, let it rest. Incubation is such an important part of the creative, intuitive process. Plant the seed and let it be!

Since intuition and the creative process are so intimately linked, let's look at how creative people create: they visualize and this process is an art form.

Shakti Gawain, author of inspirational books and pioneer in spiritual growth and consciousness once said: "We each have the truth within us. If we learn to trust, to listen to our intuition and to trust our inner knowingness, and to live by it moment by moment, then there's an inner guidance and intelligence within us that simply shows us every step of the way".

How do we close that door to intuition? We do that by distrusting our intuition, questioning its rationale, by being afraid of our own truth. Fear slams that door shut and the best way to open it again is by being loving to ourselves, encourage our own gut feelings to surface again and by being compassionate with our own shortcomings. It takes discipline to allow intuition to come through.

It's like preparing the house for the arrival of the guest: you clean it, make sure you have clean sheets, flowers, a stocked refrigerator. It takes discipline and effort to prepare...And then the guest comes.

Take a risk, trust and follow...Take a risk on your intuition in a small way: do something about your heart's desire...

Per Shakti Gawain:"As you try doing those unusual things and trusting your feelings, if you're following your intuition there will be a feeling of more aliveness. That's how you can tell. There's more juice, there's more energy, there's more aliveness that starts to happen. And when you get that feeling of more power, more aliveness, more energy, you start to be able to recognize the difference between that and a sort of deadness that happens when you don't trust yourself and don't do what you really feel. That becomes your monitoring system."

Intuitive insights can come moment by moment. One cannot set one's life on auto pilot and then not follow one's intuitive compass day by day.

This requires a shift from the head to the gut. Breathing, relaxing and checking in with your gut. Your body is your ally in this. The body wants you to connect with your gut, and when you ignore your gut, your body gets sick, overloaded, exhausted, out of alignment and it manifests in different ways...

One has to have the confidence and willingness to apply discipline and practice opening the door to intuition.

How can you continue to cultivate intuition?

Keep inviting it in with questions like: What do I need to know about A, B, C? Additionally, respect your own story, your own song and all its imperfections...Here you are in earth school, with lessons to learn and karma to work out. Intuition is your ally in this cosmic endeavor! It cuts through crusty assumptions based on semi logical assessments of a situation and goes straight to the source.

Healing can take place through intuition versus dissection of a problem through the linear mind. The linear, logical mind thinks only in duality, right versus wrong, whereas intuition allows for layers of truths as one is capable of facing. Discovering and speaking the truth and being right are two distinctly different things.

The intuitive mind comes through in metaphors whereas the linear logical mind looks at the metaphor in terms of right or wrong and tends to take metaphors literally -hence its limitations. The intuitive mind comes through a feeling in your body, trying to convey something...

This reminds me of the winter a few years ago. We have just spent another wonderful Christmas at the house in North Carolina. As I was cleaning up the place, I started getting this anxious feeling in the pit of my stomach. Walking around, tidying the place up, I found myself locking things up, securing things. I felt the need to protect this place and did not know from what. Two weeks later as I called a neighbor and asked him to measure out my master bath room for a new vanity I get the call back: "I am standing in up to one foot of water in your bedroom". Pipes broke and the entire house was under water. Now that anxious feeling made sense.

Intuitive insights pop into our consciousness: they come through feelings, vision, images, picture, and metaphors and since they pop seemingly out of nowhere they often feel like little gifts: powerful emotions come through, empathy with another comes through, art comes through, a vision for a new business venture comes through, the calling for a new book comes through. The right brain is where genius comes from.

This popping in may feel to the logical mind as very unpredictable; the logical mind feels out of control when these insights pop in, they are perceived as somewhat magical.

The linear mind is a good tool for sorting tangible reality, and the intuitive mind taps into divine knowing and brings down wisdom and deep insights into what a logical mind could only dissect but not fully understand. One needs to be willing to be vulnerable. Be open and in that openness the guest appears. We are spiritual beings who long to be in touch with the Source, the Divine, God, and the Higher Intelligence. That's what intuition ultimately is: a connection to the Source.

Being intuitive means giving up control, surrendering while paying close attention to what we feel, sense...

Have you ever played with the idea of guessing who was calling you when the phone rang? Or have you ever wondered about the "coincidence" of you hearing from a friend you just thought of? There is no such things as "coincidence" just synchronicity of energy.

So how do you best nurture your intuition?

Relax, let your mind drift, and ask for guidance with a project. Keep your linear thinking at bay, stay emotionally neutral: not too excited about anything, not upset, anxious, angry or worried...That requires self observation, listening in and tuning out all the unnecessary clutter of the mind.

What works for me is keeping a kind hearted, relaxed, open mind, with gratitude for things to come. Ask and then pay close attention to the process: who do you meet, what do they say, what does a bill board say by the side of the road, a license plate on a car in front of you, a place in the book you just cracked open...

A friend of mine once shared with me how she felt so lost when her father died; she was in mourning, crying on the way to work and wishing she could talk to her father one more time. Her father used to affectionately call her "pookie". As she was wiping her tears, driving and feeling sad a car cut in front of her and annoyed her to no end. As she looked up and saw the license plate she cracked up laughing, reading POOKIE. Tears gave way to a wistful smile as she felt the instant presence of her father.

Remember: Anything is possible when you keep your eyes wide open and allow your soul to receive the message you so need to hear.

Ask and you shall receive!!! Your Higher Self stands at a ready to provide guidance through intuitive hunches.

Instantly, my friend received the message of connection to her father; instantly, my other friend "found" the right person in a gym that lead to employment. As instant as these intuitive messages are it takes time to cultivate the frame of mind, heart and soul to allow the guest in and to understand correctly the message the guest brings with him...

When you are in the flow, things happen, your needs are instantly heard and guidance comes instantly and effortlessly.

Does that mean we should abandon logic and rational thinking, planning and seeking measurable answers? No, not at all. The intuitive process only enhances your search for achieving goals; it only guides you past rational strategies directly to the point of contact.

Logic and rational thinking are still important but you may cut down the agony of beating these tools to death once you discover the guest. Clarity comes to you before all the rational steps are exhausted and you know it is right!!!

Now, that you know how to set the ground work for the guest, how do you keep that invitation alive: how do you nurture your intuition?

Make a list of recent intuitive messages that were a successful link.

Did they come through a vivid dream, a sudden hunch, a person telling you what you needed to hear, a bill board carrying the message you were seeking?

Not only be a creator but an innovator. Put your new ideas into motion. Place them not just on paper, but on the ground.

Initially, feeling frustrated about not immediately being able to tap into one's own intuitive reservoir is normal. All things worth achieving take time and effort. Remember your old fear and doubt may want to nix a sense of guidance you received in a dream.

Also, remember, be patient, cultivate this self awareness like a precious commodity: it is your gateway to spiritual growth and joy! The power of intuitional intelligence may put you on touch with the concept of reciprocity: Confucius said: "What you do not want done to yourself, do not do to others". To avoid having negative thoughts that lead to negative actions in the future we need to observe and control our own thoughts and behaviors and cancel out our own negative attitudes. We can then encourage positive thoughts that lead to positive actions.

There is tremendous power in practice: basically any positive action with good intention can be used as practice.

Once your vision is manifested, has taken shape and has materialized, enjoy it. Allow your new creation to bless you with enjoyment, a sense of satisfaction and lightheartedness. Let it give you back meaning.

And when it's time to discontinue that creation you will know as well. Approach this part of the process with the trust of a new creation coming. You may help yourself to letting an old action go by envisioning you could live another 100 years: what would you want to do in the next ten years, given a healthy body. What would be your soul's desire? What keeps you from doing it, starting tomorrow? How can I change the perceived factors that hinder me in creating this new life? Which factors can I change? Which factors need to be looked at differently? Perception, my interpretation of these factors is key to removing perceived barriers.

So how do you stay in the natural flow?

Intuition can be blocked by a fear and doubt world view, by way of a sarcastic stance, and by way of giving up your personal power to subconscious programming.

Returning to compassion, love and trust opens the doors to being in the natural flow. As much as your understanding of intuitive awareness has grown, it takes daily enforcement that intuition—the guest—will appear as soon as you are loving, mindful, aware of your emotions and can maintain a neutral ground of humility, open mindedness, and receptiveness.

So what are the errors of judgment we all may make when it comes to intuitive awareness?

We all are reluctant to face our fears and dark sides; some of us want to race right through this territory with such great speed as to never to remember a thing. I compare that to racing down a zip line between two high posts. If you close your eyes and pretend you are not there, you do not have to face your fears.

The other pitfall is to succumb to linear thinking, to believe in this sarcastic frame of mind that diminishes and de validates the most soul based alignments and questions the higher values with the interrogation skills of a crime detector. So what happens when you fall off natural flow? You may deter your own spiritual growth; you may stall other people's spiritual growth and that is a karmic responsibility to be taken seriously...

As we embark on the spiritual path of enhancing our intuitive intelligence we will need to flex our character muscles: Is my intention of connecting intuitively to the wisdom of the Divine genuine? Or are we pursuing ego enhancement? Are we humble and genuine in our quest or are we just seeking quick answers to superficial problems?

When using your intuition practice the highest level of ethics: choose right motives, right speech and right action. Be humble, allow only the most harmless motivation to drive your quest for intuitive wisdom and use the intuition received to the highest good of all involved. Respect and honor your own wisdom and your own path.

There is no one like you in the universe; your path is unique, you are unique and your journey through this life time is like no one else's.

Bring respect and humility to all people, animals and plants when acting upon your intuitive insights. Respect other's boundaries and uniqueness.

Above all else chose your words wisely: Speech is powerful. It has the power of bringing a vision to life, of manifesting the imagined concept. Chose positive statements, use language that holds empowering messages and stay away from negative comments, complains and gossip. Negativity in speech can reduce life energy, can fester depression and anguish. Beware of your spoken word: think before you speak! You hold the power of upliftment and hope and you hold the power of truth or put downs.

And remain open to other people's perspectives: you may grow from an insight and others may need to hear your perspective to grow. Life is a journey where we alternate between giving and receiving. Give abundantly when you are moved to do so and accept help when you need it. This keeps you in the natural flow of things.

NURTURING YOUR INTUITION:

Here are 5 ways to nurture and optimize your intuitive powers:

1. Take time for silence, for meditation and reflection.

Sit quietly, take a few deep breaths, listen to soothing nature inspired music.

2. Surround yourself with a serene environment.

Find a place in your home, your back yard, in the mountains, at the beach to be, to breathe, to walk in silence, to take in that serenity.

3. Find activities and hobbies that promote introspection.

Take long walks, get a soothing massage, take a soothing bath; take long drives in your car. Try out painting, or any other art form never tried before. Do yoga or tai chi.

4. Seek the company of intuitive people.

Meet often with friends and special people and share with them your recent intuitive insights and inspirations for action. Discuss vivid meaningful dreams...

5. Maintain an open mind; pay attention to your enthusiasm.

With a curious attitude towards life one cannot be judgmental. So engage in spontaneous brain storming sessions. Use it or lose it goes for intuition as well. Use a mantra to remind you of your innate intuitive capabilities. Your enthusiasm is an indicator of your creativity being awakened by your intuition. Intuition is the seed to the creative act.

Intuitional intelligence is the way of the future. It will trigger profound changes within and without ourselves. We will relate differently to ourselves and to one another. Reality will manifest differently when we use our intuitive intelligence.

With intuitive intelligence we can remain effortlessly in the flow; resistance is futile and there is not much need to invest in paranoia, distrust and ignorance. Intuitive knowing will open doors to our innermost chambers, will allow us to receive divine wisdom without the distortions of the linear, logical thinking and will quicken our spiritual growth.

I believe your soul has a vision for this life time and intuition will spell out that vision instantly.

ABOUT THE AUTHOR

Growing up in Communist Romania, Elisabeth Mandt has started taking interest in ancient wisdom since her early adult life. Upon her family's immigration to Germany, she continued to seek answers to the meaning of life, explored meditation, sought to understand reincarnation and the natural laws of the universe.

As a licensed clinical social worker her professional involvement has spanned across various aspects of mental health and human functioning. Writing about intuition seems to be a natural extension to her daily work with transplant patients facing huge health challenges that require an inordinate amount of inner strength and coping skills.

Married for over 20 years, the author lives with her husband and her teen daughter in North East Florida and enjoys many family vacations in their North Carolina mountain house.

BIBLIOGRAPHY

AND SUGGESTED READING:

Bach, Richard, Illusions: The Adventures of a Reluctant Messiah. Dell Publishing/Random House, Inc., 1977.

Cayce, Edgar, Dreams: Your Magic Mirror, Warner Communication, New York, 1974.

Dyer, Wayne, Dr., Real Magic, Harper Collins, New York, 1992.

Gawain, Shakti, Creative Visualization, New World Library, New York, 2000.

Gawain, Shakti, Developing Intuition, New World Library; New York, 2008.

Mishlove, Jeffrey, PhD, The Intuition Network.org, founded 1986.

Osho, Intuition: Knowing Beyond Logic; St. Martin's Press, USA.

Peirce Penney, The Intuitive Way, MJF Books, New York, 1997.

Rumi: Mystical Poems of Rumi, Ibex Publishers, second edition, 2002.

Thorndike, R. L., Factor Analysis of Social and Abstract Intelligence. Journal of Educational Psychology, 1936.

Tweedie, Irina, Daughter of Fire: A Diary of a Spiritual Training with a Sufi Master, The Golden Sufi Center, 1978.

www.ingramcontent.com/pod-product-compliance
Lightning Source LLC
Chambersburg PA
CBHW031257280526
45784CB00004B/1879